1981

Cry Softly!
The Story of Child Abuse

Cry Softly!
The Story
of Child Abuse

Margaret O. Hyde

𝒲

The Westminster Press
Philadelphia

First edition

Published by The Westminster Press®
Philadelphia, Pennsylvania

PRINTED IN THE UNITED STATES OF AMERICA
9 8 7 6 5 4 3 2 1

Library of Congress Cataloging in Publication Data

Hyde, Margaret Oldroyd, 1917–
  Cry softly!

  SUMMARY: Discusses child abuse, its history in England and America, ways to prevent and stop it, and how to report suspected cases.
  1. Child abuse—Juvenile literature. 2. Child abuse—History—Juvenile literature. [1. Child abuse.] I. Title.
HV713.H98   362.7'1   80–16465
ISBN 0–664–32666–8

362.71
H994

Contents

93898

1

Cry Softly So No One Will Notice

One of the biggest secrets of the world around you is the secret that hides the abused child. A mother throws her two-year-old son across the room so hard that he hits the wall with a force that bruises him. The boy screams, and the mother tells him to cry softly so that the neighbors will not hear.

The act that hurt the child was the mother's way of punishing him. It was not the first time that he was bruised. It seldom is. A mother who batters her child needs help. Everyone knows that the child needs help, but the neighbors may not notice. They seldom do.

More and more people know about the problem of child abuse than ever before. More people are doing something to help, but most people do not know what to do. They do not understand the problem. If they did, they would care more than they do. Perhaps more of them would help.

You can learn about child abuse and share with others what you find out. No one likes to believe that babies, little children, and even teenagers are being mistreated by their parents and others who care for them. Everyone loves a child, but not all the time. In some families, the hate and ignorance come out in ways that hurt. As you learn more about the problem of child abuse, you will find that the hurt reaches out to everyone.

The hurt is especially close for Barbara. Her friend Sarah is often punished in an unusual way. Sarah's mother ties her to the bed whenever she thinks Sarah has misbehaved. Sometimes her mother tells Sarah that she is going out for just a few minutes and will untie her when she comes back.

One day when Barbara went to visit Sarah she found that her friend had been tied to the bed for several hours. Sarah said that her mother must have gone to a party and forgotten that she was still tied. Barbara felt that there must be something to do to protect her friend. She suggested telling the policewoman who was the crossing guard near school.

Sarah thought about asking the police to help her, but she was afraid that they would take her away and make her live in a strange place. Even though her mother punished her too severely, Sarah loved her. Certainly, she did not want to leave home.

How sad that neither Sarah nor Barbara knew that people trained to help with such problems try every way to prevent separating children from their families. How sad that they did not know how to ask for help.

If you think you are being mistreated, do you know how to get help? Do you think you know an abused child? Just what is child abuse? Actually, there are many kinds. Physical abuse is just one of them.

Signs of physical battering are more obvious than other kinds of abuse. Even if the child cries softly, continued physical abuse may sooner or later result in the kind of injury that makes it necessary to take a child to a doctor or a hospital.

Today, many doctors are alert for the signs of abuse. Suppose a baby is taken to an emergency room with a severe burn in the diaper area. The father explains that he dropped the little boy in a tub of very hot water, but the doctor does not see any splash marks where the hot water would have burned irregular areas of the skin if the child had been dropped. It appears that the baby was held in scalding hot water, maybe to punish him for soiling himself.

Today more doctors, nurses, social workers, teachers, and others who come in contact with children are alert to signs of battering than ever before. Children whose signs of physical abuse are serious enough may be recognized and helped, if those who notice take action.

Today we know that battered children make up only one group of abused children. Emotional abuse is another problem. This is often hurting with words. For example, a mother of twins swears at her children whenever she talks to them. These are the words that the children learn and when they talk, they talk in a language unlike that of other children.

A child may be abused emotionally by the *way* a parent talks as well as by what a parent says. Rejection may be expressed silently. Or a parent may find fault with the child again and again. Suppose a mother is cold and rejecting. If her interests are entirely selfish, the behavior of the child is not important to her. One or more of these traits may cause a type of behavior in a child that keeps him or her from growing normally.

When Sammy was four years old, he rocked back and forth hour after hour. He did not seem to learn very fast. Other children his age could talk, but Sammy said very few words. He was unusually shy when other children came to his house. His mother scolded him again and again. She was annoyed with him because he did not talk the way other boys and girls did. Why did Sammy rock all the time the way some babies do? She was sure that Sammy was retarded and this annoyed her. So she spoke to him less and less.

No one told Sammy to cry quietly. He just didn't cry at all. Sammy's mother never hit him or hurt him physically. She just could not stand being around him anymore, so she found a job and took Sammy to a day care center. There he watched other children at play and listened to them. He let other children poke at him and he never objected. He was still shy. But a day care worker took a special interest in Sammy. She talked to him and played games with him. After a while, Sammy began to talk to the lady at the day care center, but when he went home, he just rocked back and forth without saying anything. Tests showed that Sammy was not retarded. He was emotionally abused.

Many children who are emotionally abused are not so lucky as Sammy, who found a substitute mother at a day care center. Their hurt shows in many different ways. Some boys and girls seem very bright, but they are hard to get along with. They cause trouble for other children, are demanding, and act in other unpleasant ways. Of course, children may do these things for reasons other than abuse. It is very hard to know if a child is being mistreated by a mother who withholds love or treats the child in some other hurting way.

Physical neglect, like physical abuse, is a kind of child abuse that is easier to see than emotional hurt. While many children get clean clothes dirty in a very short time, it is easy to recognize clothing that has been dirty for a long time. A child who wears the wrong clothes for the weather, or who is left alone or in the care of children too young to be responsible, or who needs medical attention may be a child suffering from neglect. Neglect is a case of hurt from things not done. Many experts believe that the true number of neglect cases is far greater than other kinds of abuse and that much neglect is not counted when people try to count how many children are abused.

Another kind of child abuse is sexual mistreatment. When this happens in the home, it is usually a family secret. Many children do not even know when they have been sexually molested. For example, a parent or a baby-sitter or other person who is caring for a child may tell the child that they are playing a game and to keep the game a secret. Sally's father had begun to fondle her while bathing her when she was very young. Gradually, he introduced her to his sexual desires. In her sixth-grade classroom when Sally discussed the games she played with her father, she had no idea that other children did not act the same way with their fathers.

Many children are sexually abused in less subtle ways, against their wishes. One of the common reasons given for running away is sexual advances by a member of the family.

What is child abuse? According to the United States Congress, it is "the physical or mental injury, sexual abuse, negligent treatment or maltreatment of a child under the age of eighteen by a person who is responsible for the child's welfare under circumstances which indicate that the child's health or welfare is harmed or threatened thereby."

A number of definitions of child abuse show growing understanding for the abuser. One is "a family crisis which threatens the physical or emotional survival of a child." Such views are the result of an effort to identify the causes of the problem as well as to treat the symptoms of the child. So, it might be possible to help the family in such a way that the abuse would not continue to happen. Since abuse is seldom just a single happening from the simple burst of rage of a parent, the problem is far deeper than healing a broken leg or other easily seen injury.

Perhaps no mother wakes up thinking that she is going to batter her child. Who would do such a horrible thing? A father who punishes his child by burning an arm with his cigarette probably does not know that there are better ways to teach about fire. Who are these people who tell their children to cry quietly so the neighbors will not hear them?

2

Who Are
the Child Abusers?

If you stood in a crowd of people and looked around, you could not pick out the child abusers. When one sees pictures of children who have been battered, it is easy to think of the parents who abused them as monsters.

Are these people suffering from a mental illness that distorts their thinking? Are they mean people who cannot understand that hurting children is a horrid thing to do? What causes people to abuse their children? Why would anyone behave this way?

You may know child abusers without realizing it. They come from all kinds of society. They belong to all races, religions, age groups, and to both sexes. A child abuser may be the man who lives down the street. Call him Mr. Jones. He goes to work each day, speaks pleasantly, but shyly, to you when you meet him on the street, and looks like a person who could never harm any kind of living thing. Inside the house, this man is part of a family under stress. He never felt loved as a child, and he was unable to love his own children. One of the children, Mary, was especially troublesome as far as Mr. Jones was concerned. She looked somewhat like the sister he had always hated, and she was born at a time when he was under great stress at work. She always seemed to be crying when he came home from work. Why couldn't Mary behave? Why couldn't she show how much she loved him? His sister never showed any love for him, and this child was going to be just like her.

Actually, Mr. Jones expected too much of Mary. He expected her to provide the love he missed as a child, and he could not understand that Mary was too young to provide grown-up comfort and love.

When Mr. Jones beat Mary, she cried even more. The mother tried to protect the child, but she felt her first duty was to her husband. She decided that Mary was young and she would forget the severe beatings. Her body would heal fast. When people asked about the bruises on Mary's body, the mother found excuses for them. Most of the time, she could cover the red marks with clothing.

Mr. Jones continues to pass as a fine, considerate

man. Certainly he is not a monster. He does not willfully hurt his child.

What kind of person would harm a child? Certainly there must be many abusive parents and just as certainly, each person and each case is different from every other one.

In their efforts to prevent abuse, many men and women who study this problem have suggested traits that are common among child abusers. This does not mean that everyone with these traits is a child abuser or that a child abuser must have all these traits.

Less than ten percent of the people who hurt children are so severely troubled that there is little chance of helping them to overcome their problem. Some of this ten percent do not live in the real world, but in a world that exists only in their imaginations. Some hear voices and are very confused in their thinking. The child may be considered as a force of the devil, as a threat, or in some other unreal way. A very severely depressed parent may not have the energy or the ability to take care of a child. This is one reason for neglect.

It has been suggested that child abuse is one way people have of asking for help. Abusive parents are usually unable to reach out for help the way most people can, for they have lost their sense of community and their sense of trust. Many are loners who have nothing to do with their neighbors, have no other family nearby and no real friends with whom they can discuss their problems. In some cases, living in a country place, far from other people, seems to play a part in child abuse.

People who hurt their children again and again are apt to have a poor opinion of themselves, to feel that they have failed in most everything they have tried, and to feel that they have little to offer the world. Perhaps as a result of this they expect too much of their children. If they have not been successful, they hope that their children will be winners, and that will make them proud. They want to enjoy the reflected glory of their children's success, so they push the children very hard, often beyond what they can do. Parents treat these children as if they were older than they really are.

In some cases, parents really don't know what can be expected of children at various ages. June was a six-week-old baby when her father decided she should learn not to cry when he wanted her to be quiet. He punished her when she did not stop crying by spanking her. The more he hit her, the more she cried. In a fit of temper, he broke her ribs.

Many parents who were unloved or felt unloved as children look to their young as a source of comfort and loving response. They act like children themselves and seem to consider their children as adults. They try to gain a parent when they have a child. This is known as "role reversal." Since the child cannot succeed in the impossible role of an adult, the parent feels rejected again. Feelings of dependence, rage, and depression are acted out in beatings or other kinds of mistreatment.

Most parents have high hopes for their children as they look to the future. When parents hurt children who do not live up to their hopes, they are expecting the children to act like adults long before reaching that period in life. Part of this may be due to feelings of hate toward the parent's own past that alters understanding of the children's limited abilities and helplessness. What happens is twisted by the parent's own past experiences.

Sometimes fantasy in the form of role reversal takes place at the time of an attack on a child. A parent may imagine that the child is a nagging, critical mother or father from long ago. The parent, who does not know how to express feelings safely, strikes out at the child.

In most cases of role reversal, the parent was never able to secure love and support from his or her own parents or from other human beings during childhood. Karen's case shows this.

Karen brought her five-week-old baby to the hospital with bruises on his face. She explained that she had hit the baby because he did not love her. No one had ever loved her, and she had waited a long time for a baby who would. When the baby cried, she felt that he did not love her, so she hit him each time he cried.

Some parents are just not interested in their children. They may be especially irritated by a child who cries a great deal, or they may have very little patience. A television producer may lash out at a child who interferes with the work he brought home to meet an important schedule. He has no interest in any children, least of all his own child, who always seems to be demanding time he needs for his career.

One trait that many child abusers share is an inability to act appropriately to the seriousness of a problem. They strike out at children to relieve unbearable pressures. Whether they are rich or poor, the stress brings out any weaknesses in their personalities.

Bertha is a parent under stress. She works all day at a house where there is every comfort. At home, she makes dinner for her five children in a kitchen that has no counter space and no hot water. She tries to keep the house clean, but there are no closets, and everything always seems to be all over the place. The children have a hard time understanding poverty. They want the things that they see advertised on the old television set that someone gave their mother. They cannot understand why she will not buy them.

One of Bertha's children is especially troublesome. Bertha watches him as he leans out the window. She feels like pushing him out. When he picks up her favorite ashtray and throws it out the window at a passing dog, Bertha hits him with a chair.

Bertha is sorry she hit her son, but she has just suffered too much this day. It is more than she can bear. She has always been too proud to ask for help, since she thinks that that means she is weak. She is overwhelmed with being a parent, and now she is a child abuser. The stress is just too much.

Confusion between discipline and abuse is a problem for some parents. Many people have a fear of spoiling a child or believe that one should not give in to a child.

John's father was careful to show him who was boss. He told his friends that John was not going to be allowed to get away with some things the way other children could. He would be a strong parent. While he was trying to discipline John, his actions sometimes got out of hand and he would hurt more than he meant to hurt. When John upset his father's beer two times in one afternoon, the father exploded with anger. The only way to teach this clumsy child was to beat him, and even then he never seemed to learn. His father beat John until three ribs were broken.

Most abusing parents love their children and feel very upset when they discover that they have done something to harm a child. But they continue to lash out at their children when they feel that they are not getting anywhere with their attempts at discipline. This is especially true when a parent does not know what to expect from a child at various ages.

Tim was only sixteen months old when his mother took him to the hospital because he had a "sore ear." When asked how the injury had happened, she explained that she was teaching Tim to come when he was called. When he did not obey, she tugged gently on his ear to remind him that he was supposed to do what she told him. Doctors at the hospital found that the ear was partly torn away from the child's head.

While some people who study the problem feel that there is more child abuse among poor people than among others, many disagree. They claim that the lives of poor people are more exposed to individuals who notice abuse. For example, welfare workers, social workers, day care workers, and others see more poor children under school age than children of the middle class and the wealthy. People who can afford private help for their problems may never be included in the reports. Yet many poor people do suffer from more stress just in order to survive. No one really knows the truth in this argument, but one thing is certain, children in some families in all kinds of social situations suffer from abuse.

One of the most common characteristics of people who abuse their children is believed to be their
own abuse when they were young. Much of how
one behaves as a parent is learned from how one
was treated as a child. This is why one often hears
the expression "the cycle of abuse." Children who
have been hurt are apt to hurt their own children,
and when these children grow up, they may continue the pattern. However, not all people who
have been abused continue this kind of parenting.

The causes of abuse are many. New approaches
to helping children who are mistreated and neglected include help for parents, too. Many doctors
who see severely battered children try to understand why a parent has treated a child in such an
ugly way. They must also consider whether or not
it is safe to let the healed child go home with these
parents. Getting the parents to accept help with
their problems so the child will not continue to be
abused is part of the healing process.

Many people who abuse their children see life as
something done to them rather than something
they can manage. Things may be terrible for them,
but they are resigned to it. "That's the way life is"
is a common expression among people who do not
know how to cope. But while they accept life as it
is, they have difficulty controlling their anger and
rage.

Most parents engage in some form of abuse at

least one time in their lives, but this does not mean that they are abusive parents. If hurting a child is repeated and becomes a pattern of behavior, a parent has an abuse problem. Certainly, there are many forms of abuse and many different kinds of parents who abuse their children.

While child abusers may have many characteristics in common, there are only two that all of them share: (1) They hurt their children. (2) They need help.

3

Who Are the Crying Children?

Some children are more likely to be mistreated than others, and often no one knows exactly why. In a family where one of the parents is a child abuser, it usually happens that only one child of many is the one to suffer. This special child is the one that a parent sees as different from the other children.

Actually, the child may be different. He or she may have a birth defect, may be retarded, may be particularly active, may have a speech defect, may look like a hated relative, or have any of a wide variety of traits that peg the child as different. Sometimes it may be that the child is not the sex that the parents wanted. Or the child might have red hair instead of the blond hair they considered nicer.

Jim was the fifth child in a family of easygoing children. His temperament was different. Even during the first five weeks, his mother found that he hated new things. When she bathed him, an especially happy time for her other children, Jim screamed. He never cried softly, he always screamed. Jim was a "bad baby." When his mother was under stress, she blamed all her problems on Jim. He was the child who took the verbal abuse.

Jim and other abused children are often the victims of problems that are not related to them but they are chosen, rather than brothers and sisters, for some reason that makes them special.

Some children seem like little adults because they learn to fill their parents' needs for love and comfort at an early age. They take care of the parents instead of the parents taking care of them. Such a child develops a tendency to yield to others, a kind of behavior that is not usual for children. This boy or girl is deprived of a normal childhood. Also, he or she learns never to trust anyone. No one provides comfort or satisfies the child's need to feel safe.

In one family, a four-year-old child is always alert for the cries of her eighteen-month-old sister. She feeds her, comforts her when she cries, and takes her along wherever she goes. The four-year-old gets no positive feelings from her abusive mother, but she does develop some self-esteem through her care of her younger sister. This is at the expense of her own normal childhood and of her emotional health when she becomes an adult.

Paul has an unhappy situation at home. His mother is especially upset by any criticism, a long-standing condition that goes back to her childhood when her own father rejected her. She fears being rejected by all men, and she has been unable to form a good relationship with her husband. She uses Paul as a substitute man around the house. He takes care of his younger brothers and sisters, helps his mother buy food, and cooks. When his mother goes out in the evenings, Paul goes with her in place of his father. His mother needs to depend on him so much that he is not permitted his own need to be dependent. He may well grow up to be an abusing parent. Deprived of the care he needed when he was young, he may never be able to provide it for others.

Betty is a seven-year-old who is withdrawn, underweight, and unlikable. She cannot get along with her classmates, since she is unwilling to take part in any activities in which she cannot be the boss. At home, Betty takes care of her mother, even feeding her when the mother says she is sick. Betty hoards food from the school lunch that is provided for her, and she takes it home to her mother. She knows that she will be asked the same question each day as soon as she gets home, "What did you bring me?" If Betty does not think of her mother before she thinks of herself, she is made to feel guilty. She is abused.

Twelve-year-old Sally was always afraid of her mother, a woman who would beat her with a belt that had a buckle on it. Sally did whatever her mother told her to do. She cared for her five younger brothers and sisters, staying home from school to take care of the little ones while her mother slept till noon. Sally did not enjoy her role as mother. In fact, she teased the children, was sullen and depressed. She ate a great deal and was quite fat. Much of her anger was turned against herself, but she could not escape from the hold that her mother had on her.

Even when children are very young, signs of mistreatment can often be detected by a person who knows what they are. For example, when most babies are brought to a doctor's office and placed on an examining table, they turn toward their mothers. An abused baby does not. This baby is usually fearful of being touched by any adult and may cry hopelessly while being examined. There is little or no eye contact between the parent and the baby. An abused child may appear to be alert for danger at a very young age.

When young children who have been battered are placed in a hospital, most of them do not ask to go home the way other children do. They are wary of being touched by adults and seem always to wonder what is coming next. Usually children in a hospital become interested in other children in a ward and reach out to adults for help after a short time. While some seem unafraid of being in a ward and settle in unusually fast, others exhibit "frozen watchfulness." This has been seen in children as young as nine or ten months. These abused children tend to sit or lie still, watching quietly whatever is going on around them. They may remain quietly alert for several days watching to see what is going to happen. Many ask again and again, "What is going to happen next?"

When abused children reach school age, teachers may recognize them from one or more of the following clues. These are not proof of maltreatment, since they can reflect other situations, but they are danger signs:

coming to school with dirty clothing, body odor, or unkempt appearance

having unexplained injury

acting shy, withdrawn, or too eager to cooperate

arriving at school early and leaving late

not wanting to go home

wearing long-sleeved clothes in warm weather

talking about beatings

acting nervous, too active, or destructive

acting fearful of being touched by an adult

being absent from school with poor or no ex-
cuse

showing little hope of being comforted when
in trouble

always searching for favors, food, or services

having problems in getting along with other
children.

No one of these is necessarily a sign of abuse at home, but a child showing several of them may make a teacher suspicious. An abused child is a lonely, joyless person who has little contact with people of his or her own age. You, alone, may not be able to identify an abused child, but your teacher may be alerted to recognize clues if you talk about them.

Children who are old enough to talk often deny that they have been abused, either because they feel a loyalty to parents or because they fear that they will be further abused for telling. Since they do not usually trust others, these children keep the secrets in the family.

One thing seems certain: child abuse is epidemic in the United States. No one knows exactly how many children are abused, but according to one widely accepted estimate the number is one million in a year. About two thousand children probably die each year because parents, baby-sitters, or other people who care for them, mistreat them. That means that six children will die today from abuse or neglect. One child will die every four hours.

Recently, it has been suggested that the true figure for child abuse cases is closer to two million each year than it is to one million. This is twice the number of people who live in the state of Rhode Island.

Measuring the amount of abuse is an impossible task for several reasons. First, not everyone agrees on the kinds of problems that should be included. When neglect is counted, the numbers are much larger. Second, a great many cases are never reported. Third, there is no way of knowing how much abuse actually happens. The nature of mistreatment makes it a very private action and since even the kind of physical abuse that needs medical attention can be similar to injuries from accidents, abuse is hard to detect.

Experts try to learn how much abuse there is in a variety of ways. Some studies are based on reports made by people who were asked to recall whether or not they were abused as children. Large numbers of people are involved and the results are adjusted to show how many would be reported if the study had been based on the population of the whole United States. No one claims that the numbers are accurate, but this is one way to get some idea of the extent of abuse and neglect.

Dr. Richard Gelles, a professor at the University of Rhode Island, has recently conducted a study of families throughout the United States. He has reached the conclusion that about four out of every one hundred children under the age of seventeen are being abused or neglected.

The Texas Council of Child Welfare Boards explored the problem of child abuse in their state in 1979. One person in seven reported experiencing abuse or neglect in their childhood. Only one in four of these people had told about their problems as a child because they were afraid that they would be hurt more if they told. Some did not know where to report it, and others thought that everyone was treated the same way until they grew up and found that what had happened to them was not usual.

Dr. David Gil, of Brandeis University, based his idea of the number of abused children on about thirteen thousand case reports. In over half of these cases, the abuse resulted from angry parents punishing children for real misconduct or what they considered real. Based on this, as many as two million children may be abused each year, although there is no way of being accurate.

The number of children who die each year as the

result of abuse is hard to determine, too. Dr. Vincent J. Fontana, an expert on child abuse, suggests that there are seven hundred hurt children a year. Many who study the problem feel certain that at least one child dies every day. The number may be much greater. Dr. Ray E. Helfer, in his testimony before a subcommittee of the United States Senate in 1973, said that he believed there would be over five thousand child deaths a year over the following ten years if steps were not taken to curb abuse.

Many experts agree with the figure suggested by the National Center on Child Abuse and Neglect —one million cases of abuse a year and six deaths a day. If we think in terms of large numbers, the abuse seems less real. If we consider the death of one battered child, it becomes a tragedy.

4

Children of
Very Long Ago

Child abuse is not new. If you lived long ago, your chances of being hurt would have been much greater than they are today. Infanticide, the killing of young babies, was a widely accepted practice in many parts of the world. Infanticide, in olden times, was not considered murder because it was killing with consent of the parent, family, or community. In some cases, the reason was simply not enough food for a large family. In some cultures, any child born after the third was either killed or eliminated by being sold or abandoned.

Children born out of wedlock were often the victims of infanticide because of dishonor, poor care, or the economic plight of the mother. Many illegitimate babies were abandoned. Since the infant almost always died, this usually amounted to infanticide. Some infants were placed in the care of nurses, who collected a fee and then did away with them. Many children were kept to be used for begging on the streets for money they had to turn over to the adults.

Sacrificing a child to the gods was common in ancient times. The case of Abraham, who offered his son Isaac as a sacrifice but whose hand was stayed by divine intervention, is better known and has a happier ending than most cases. In some cultures, the firstborn son was always sacrificed, while in others the firstborn son was allowed to live but other sons were not. This prevented problems about who would inherit the family's possessions.

Children who were weak, had birth defects, were girls, or who were unwanted for some other reason were put to death soon after birth. If you think about the reasons for infanticide, you will not find it difficult to believe that babies were not valued long ago as they are in today's world. Although there are rare occasions in which mothers dispose of their children in modern times, these are punishable as serious crimes.

Were there other kinds of abuse in times gone by? How were the children who lived treated in early times? One hopes that many of them were loved, but records show that it was not uncommon for parents to abandon an infant. Through the centuries, many children were left on mountainsides where wild animals would find them, in rivers where they would drown, or in any nearby place where they would starve to death or become victims of the elements. As late as the eighteenth century in England, children were left in the streets to die while people walked by with little or no concern. For centuries, many children died at an early age. One reason for widespread child abuse is thought to be the lack of feeling for a child who would probably never live to grow up. Perhaps parents were afraid to become attached to children. If they did not care about them, they would not suffer when they were lost.

Another factor in child abuse was the parent-child relationship. In general, the lot of boys and girls throughout history was a hard one. From one era to the next, generation after generation, the child was the property of the father to do with as he wished. This was written into law in the Code of Hammurabi, which was based on early Babylonian law, dating back to 2130 B.C. According to the code, a man was free to give his child (or wife) in payment of a debt. The child could be sold or exchanged for goods. In days gone by, being sold into slavery was a form of abuse that many children had to endure.

Codes that followed this earliest set of laws included similar powers for fathers. The child was property of the father, who was entitled to absolute respect. While children made out somewhat better during the height of Greek civilization, about five hundred years before the birth of Christ, these attitudes later disappeared.

Even in early Greece, fathers would decide whether or not a baby would be allowed to live or die. In the upper classes, the child was laid at a man's feet soon after birth. If he picked it up, the child was accepted and allowed to live, but if he turned away from it, a slave disposed of the child by placing it in a large jar, or throwing it into a manure heap or a river. Aristotle wrote that "the justice of a master or a father is a different thing from that of a citizen, for a son or slave is property, and there can be no injustice to one's own property."

Sometimes, babies were left where people would see them, with the hope that they would be adopted. A precious stone or something of value might be tied to the baby, perhaps to make a person who saw it believe that adoption would bring good luck. Child abuse was often the next thing in store for these babies. Adults plucked out eyes, twisted legs, cut off hands and feet of the babies and sent them, as little children, out to beg. Young beggars who were deformed caused both pity and amusement to some adults in ancient times. Attitudes about children have changed so much since that time that today it is difficult to imagine deliberately harming a child for the sake of a few more pennies.

Through the years, people paid no attention to

the mistreatment and suffering of children. This was true of people who saw the children, of people who knew them, and, in many cases, of their parents. Some children were treated with love and kindness, but this attention was often at the whim of the parents. Everyone was used to seeing children abused. This was the custom for many years. This was the way life was. Survival was difficult for most adults, and little attempt was made to soften life for children.

Much of the indifference and cruelty to children was probably due to ignorance of conditions necessary for their well-being. Superstitions were the basis of much that passed for care. A child who was born under a curse carried that curse for a lifetime.

In much of the period known as the Middle Ages (roughly A.D. 500–1500) children continued to suffer. In some houses, children slept on the floor with domestic animals. They shared the dirt, the worms, and the diseases. People did not consider this child abuse, for no one knew any better. Children of wealthy parents slept on the floor of the great hall with the servants, and all of them were considered on a level with servants.

Poor children worked along with their parents when they were barely more than infants. All children worked for the manor or the community beginning at an early age. Family life, in which a mother, father, and children were a unit, was not known until the seventeenth century.

It was common for children over seven to learn through serving a family other than their own in what was known as apprenticeship. This was also called "binding out." The arrangement was made by the father, who decided where to place the child and the length of time. Children had no choice in the matter. Children of rich people were usually sent to another castle or to a church. Middle-class boys were sent to craftsmen to do their menial tasks and to learn from them, and girls were sent to other households to act as servants. Poor children were either kept with their parents, helping them with the chores necessary for their survival, or they were placed in the lowest kind of service.

No matter how they were treated, apprentices were forced to work under the arrangements made by their parents. Many children were severely beaten, and probably few escaped what would be considered severe abuse in today's world.

Children were plentiful, even though many died at an early age. According to some theories, parents considered children easier to replace than their more expensive domestic animals. This was true even though only one in two or three lived through childhood. Spoiled food, fire, and famine took their toll, along with epidemics of plague, influenza, smallpox, tuberculosis, dysentery, and typhoid.

Adults, too, suffered from these diseases and many children were orphaned at birth or in their early years. Groups of little boys and girls were put in the care of women who treated them in any way they wished. Few of these women, if any, spared the rod. Beatings were common.

During most of the Middle Ages, parents continued to neglect their children. The little attention children did receive was often a form of physical abuse. But toward the end of the Middle Ages, in the twelfth and thirteenth centuries, the status of children improved somewhat. This was partly due to the growth of chivalry and partly due to an interest in the infant Jesus. In the past, Christians had not thought of him as a typical child, but around this period, they thought of the young Jesus with more human qualities. Children, in general, were better off because of this interest.

But child abuse did not disappear. This was especially true in the case of children of the poor and children who were orphaned or disowned. Poor families continued to struggle for survival, their children working side by side with the adults at a very early age.

Beatings were still common for children in all classes. Even King Henry VI was flogged regularly by his tutor when he was growing up. Charles I was more fortunate, since he had a whipping boy who took his beatings. Even though some adults spoke up against the harsh physical abuse, children continued to be whipped. There are accounts of battered children who died as a result of beatings, but most cases probably went unnoticed.

5

Hurt Children in Yesterday's England

Early English law of about A.D. 1300 was similar to Roman law in the treatment of children. A father had complete control over the young, and in times of poverty he could sell a son or a daughter. A child could own property at this time in England and the father acted as guardian until a certain age was reached. A few hundred years later, the old Roman idea in which the state could take over the duties of parents was adopted in England. These English laws and the English laws that followed were the basis of laws in the United States.

By the sixteenth century in England, the number of poor people was so great that large numbers were starving. Many parents and their children had to beg for enough food to keep them alive. The Poor Relief Act of 1601 was passed to make work for those children whose parents could not provide for them. Thousands of children were sent from

England to work in America. As a result of the poor laws, children whose parents could not feed them were taken from them permanently. The laws did not work very well, and about fifty years later, the government of England used another system that placed children in workhouses for the poor.

Conditions in the workhouses were so bad that almost all the children sent there died. For babies less than one year old the death rate was 99 percent, and for those slightly older it was 80 percent to 90 percent. A child's chances of survival, no matter where, were still poor. Even though a family with a mother, father, and children, had evolved as a unit and parents showed more concern for their children than before, many children died before the age of five. Abuse of all sorts was still common.

The great gin-drinking period of London in the eighteenth century was one of tragedy and horror. Gin was cheap and brought forgetfulness of cold and misery. One famous case of child abuse of the time was recorded in the Sessions Papers of Old Bailey (the jail) of 1734. Judith Dufour took her two-year-old child from the workhouse where it had just been newly clothed. She pretended to take it out for the afternoon, but she strangled the child and left it in a ditch after removing the clothing. She sold the clothing for money, which she and a friend used to buy gin. Judith Dufour worked all that night in a mill, and there she confessed what she had done to another woman who worked with her. She was accused of the crime and probably punished, but many other child abusers were never recognized.

The children who were exposed in the streets of London had long been a problem for some people who had developed feelings of social concern. These people worked for years to establish the London Foundling Hospital. In 1739, the following was signed by a number of ladies of rank and presented to the government:

"No expedient has yet been found out for preventing the murder of poor miserable infants at their birth, or suppressing the inhuman custom of exposing newly-born infants to perish in the streets; or the putting of such unhappy foundlings to wicked and barbarous nurses, who undertake to bring them up for a small and trifling sum of money, do often suffer them to starve for want of due sustenance or care, or if permitted to live . . . turn them into the streets to beg or steal."

The London Foundling Hospital was established, but it could care for only a limited number of children. Further work on the part of interested and charitable people improved the lot of poor children to some degree, but there was still a great deal of hardship and cruelty.

For hundreds of years, the hours that children

worked on the farms remained about the same. In winter, they worked from dawn to dusk, and in the spring from eight to six. In harvesttime, many worked from five in the morning until nine at night. For this work, the reward was small, but it added to wages of the fathers and mothers. Children were put to work as soon as they were able to earn money, and no one saw any abuse in this way of adding to the family income.

The children who were sent to school were disciplined by flogging there as well as at home. Parents took the Bible verse "Spare the rod and spoil the child" seriously. Many parents truly believed that giving harsh beatings was part of their responsibility in raising a child. But here and there a voice was raised in defense of children, and for some children life was less harsh.

Jean Jacques Rousseau, a Frenchman, played an important part in changing attitudes about children. He recognized that there were definite periods of development in a child's life, and that a child was not just a miniature adult. But in spite of his interest and enlightened attitude, Rousseau abandoned his own children. However, his book *Émile,* published in 1762, had an important influence on child care in England. For some children, their recognition as persons meant less abuse, but this was not true for all children.

When making goods took place in homes, children helped with the chores, working long hours in cottage industries such as spinning and weaving. In the middle of the eighteenth century, around the time that George Washington was growing up in America, it was not uncommon to find English children of the ages of three and four working in the factories. Little children picked up the waste cotton from the floors. They were especially valuable as workers who could creep under the machines where older and larger people could not go.

Older children suffered a different kind of abuse. They were made to work fifteen hours a day, sometimes at night. If they refused, they were beaten. Large numbers of children worked under the pressure of this fear.

The harshness of many parents in England in the eighteenth century fills today's students of the times with horror. The laws were equally cruel. Children were among the people who were publicly hanged and in some cases the offense was trivial. For example, a little girl seven years of age was hanged in the marketplace for stealing a petticoat. Parents considered it good discipline to take their children to see the body of a murderer hanging in chains.

Jonas Hanway, who was active in protecting youngsters, protested against the abuse of children who were put to work sweeping chimneys. His concern for them is easily understood when one reads about their lot in life.

Jeff was a climbing-boy for a chimney sweep in London about two hundred years ago. He was one of many young boys who were sold or abandoned at a very young age. Jeff was told to climb up a chimney of the local church, but the area was small and he had to struggle to get into the space. His master, the sweep, sent another boy to poke him by putting his head underneath Jeff's body. At other times, during a period of two hours, Jeff was pricked by a pin fastened to the end of a stick. One time when he tried to come down, a small fire was built under him. He cleaned the chimney as best he could, but the skin was rubbed from his knees and elbows. He had perspired so much from both fear and exertion while trying to clean the chimney that his body was covered with sweat, much as if water had been thrown on him.

This actual case was reported in *The Lady's Magazine, An Entertaining Companion for the Fair Sex,* Vol. XXXXIII, in London, December 31, 1802. Many similar reports could be made, for it was well known that climbing-boys were physically abused just by the nature of their work. Not until 1788 was a bill passed in Parliament that prohibited boys under the age of eight from becoming apprentices and forbidding a sweep from having more than six boys at one time. Unfortunately for the boys, the act was almost totally ignored.

In the year 1800, The Society for Superseding the Necessity of Climbing-Boys was formed. This group tried to encourage the use of a special kind of brush that was invented at that time. But this and similar brushes were not commonly used until nearly a hundred years later.

Climbing-boys often became deformed from their work, and many who worked in the soot developed cancer. A report published at the time claimed that those who survived "came to no good." Many children were overcome by fumes and some suffocated in the chimney flues. Common treatment for the inevitable bleeding knees and elbows consisted of rubbing them with salt brine to harden the raw flesh.

Children were abused in a variety of work situations. During the eighteenth and nineteenth centuries, many children were employed in the mines, where they worked for twelve hours a day. Some of the little ones were trappers, who opened and shut trapdoors that controlled the ventilation of the mines. Children also filled the carriages with coal and pushed the trucks from the end of the tunnel to the shaft of the mine where the coal could be raised to the surface.

If you had lived at the time of Sarah Gooder, who was eight years old in 1842, you might not have thought about her situation the way you do today. But even by the standards of the time, she was considered abused by some people who took the trouble to care. Sarah described her day as a trapper in the pit of a mine, where she worked from four in the morning until half past five at night. She was "scared" in the dark. She said that she sometimes sang when she saw the daylight. She could not sing in the dark because of her fear. Sarah claimed that she never went to sleep.

The report of Sarah and of other girls who drew trucks along the paths in the coal mines was presented to the English Parliament in 1842 and resulted in a ruling against the employment of children under ten in the mines.

In the eighteenth century, apprenticeship was still the way of giving a child a start in life while using the work of that child to pay for his or her keep. In the case of poor children, the fee received for apprenticeship was low. The master might be a "tiger in cruelty." He might beat, abuse, strip naked, starve, or do what he wished with an innocent child. No one would notice.

Children were bound out, or apprenticed, to be domestic servants, were kidnapped or sent by parents to be members of gangs who worked long hours on plantations, were sent into the streets to hawk milk, and were apprenticed in a wide variety of ways.

The poor laws of the time forced a parish, or community, to pay the apprentice fee for a poor child. Placing children in another parish got rid of the obligation. In most cases, no one cared to whom or for what kind of work a child was apprenticed as long as the master lived in another parish. There were masters who secured the fee for taking an apprentice, and then got rid of the child by cruel treatment that made the child run away.

By the nineteenth century a new phase in the protection of children had begun. The movement gathered the support of many people. Certainly, child abuse was not a problem just for poor children, although they may have been victims more often. In the crusade to protect children, a "lady of position" named Mrs. Montague was convicted of manslaughter in the year 1892. She had tied up her small daughter and locked her in a cupboard for five hours. The child died. It was argued in her defense that a parent had a right to punish a child in a reasonable manner, but she was sentenced to twelve months' imprisonment.

Through the years, societies for the prevention of cruelty to children were formed in England. Prosecutions for the neglect and cruelty to children by their caretakers, including their own parents, became more frequent. People were coming to understand and appreciate the necessary conditions for human life and to realize that a child is a person, not property.

The Children Act of 1948 is considered an important law, not only because it brought together the administration of child care into a single service, but because of the idea of children's rights on which the service was based. Now it was openly agreed that all children, rich and poor alike, had the rights of support, security, health, happiness, and fulfillment. Certainly, this was not the end of all child abuse, but it was a long way from conditions of even one hundred years earlier.

6

Child Abuse: American Style

While American children generally had more freedom than those in England, child labor followed the colonists to America. The Puritans considered the work experience a proper way to train a child. Apprenticeship was practiced in colonial days, and many children were bound out to service when they were as young as four years of age.

There are records of cases in which abuse was considered serious enough to be brought to court. In Salem, Massachusetts, in the year 1630, a man was brought to trial for murdering his apprentice, but he was acquitted by a jury because they considered that the boy was "ill disposed." The jury did find the boy's punishment to be unreasonable, since it evidently caused the boy's skull to be broken. In another case, a man who killed his apprentice through a series of beatings was said to have been executed in Boston, Massachusetts, in the year

1643. Perhaps the difference between these two cases was the fact that the first incident of abuse was not part of a pattern. No one knows how many young apprentices were treated kindly or how many were abused by beatings. Probably a great many children worked for very long hours.

According to the custom, many children of colonial times were severely punished when they did not obey. The Stubborn Child Law, which was passed in Massachusetts in the year 1646, called for the death of children who were not obedient, providing their parents were not at fault. Public whipping was usually substituted, but there was no doubt about the rights of parents to force their wishes on their children. The Stubborn Child Law was finally repealed in 1973.

Parents had the right to any money that their children earned, and money earned by any children they chose to accept into their families. Many children were shipped to the colonies and were put to work under contract; but they received no wages other than their keep.

Through the centuries, some voices were raised against the plight of children who worked in factories from the time they were very young. It was pointed out that they had little chance for fresh air, play, or education. Laws were passed to protect children, but as in England, they were not strictly enforced. Many children who suffered the abuse of long hours and poor pay grew up in poverty untrained for anything better than the unskilled work they did for long hours as a child.

Child labor was accepted by the public as a service to the poor, a way for the children to help support their families. Hard work was considered a good thing, and the old saying that hard work never hurt anyone was applied without serious thought to the children as well as to adults.

The abandoned children who were too young or too sick to work were taken to almshouses, where they were assigned to the care of the poor women who were living there. As in England, conditions at the almshouses were horrid, and many of the babies who were sent there died at a very young age. Children were housed with the disabled and diseased in dirty conditions and given no education. Babies were supposed to be fed by wet nurses, women whose breasts had recently supplied milk for their own babies. These wet nurses were so much in demand that some abandoned children were sent out to live with families. Conditions in these homes were no better than in the almshouses.

During the period that followed the Civil War, times were especially bad. In New York City, there were so many babies abandoned on doorsteps, left in gutters, and thrown in trash cans that the Sisters of Charity received support in their efforts to help children. Sister Mary Irene Fitzgibbon and two other nuns opened the door of a small house to abandoned babies. This was the beginning of the New York Foundling Hospital. On October 11, 1869, the Sisters placed a small crib at the entrance of the house and let it be known through the city's newspapers that they would care for unwanted infants who were placed in the little crib.

In the days and months that followed, the crib was seldom empty. Some children were left with notes pinned to their clothing telling their names. Some were dressed in rags and some in fine clothing. A dollar or two was often found along with a baby and a note that said the mother had no more money to care for the child. Over one thousand babies were received during the first year, but at least as many were discarded in the streets over a two-year period. The New York Foundling Hospital continued to grow through the years, and it still provides help for a limited number of neglected and abused children as well as for their parents.

Since the attitude toward children in the nineteenth century continued to be one that upheld the rights of parents to punish their children as they wished, many children were cruelly treated by their parents. They had no protection under the law, but a step toward their protection was made in 1838. In that year, the Supreme Court of Pennsylvania reached the decision that the state government could, in some cases, rule to take children from parents who did not or would not care for them. This made the government guardian of these children, as it was in England.

What would happen to the wards of the state? During the last century in America, many reform schools, farm schools, orphanages and asylums of various kinds sprang into being. Children who broke the law, children who were abandoned or neglected, and children who were orphaned were housed in them. By the turn of the century there was a vast network of orphan asylums, but many orphans were still found with juvenile and adult offenders. In many cases, the neglected became the abused, and those who were not "wayward" learned from those who were living in the institutions because they had broken the law. Many children who had already suffered from abuse at home were now at the mercy of guards who used harsh discipline.

By the year 1845, some of the children who had been in orphanages and other institutions were placed in foster homes. Large numbers of children went to work for farmers, who took them into their families. In many cases, this worked out very well. But even after the slaves were freed by the Civil War, children in all parts of the country were still put to work on the farms at a very early age and made to work in the fields from sunrise to sunset.

Other children worked long hours in mines, in mills, and in factories. Even those who received some schooling were "taught to the tune of the hickory stick."

Between the years 1854 and 1875, about twenty thousand children were sent to the West to find new homes with any family who befriended them. Groups of boys and girls arrived at a destination by train and were taken to a meeting where a large crowd had gathered. The children were set apart from the group one by one, while a leader read a brief account of each child. An applicant from the crowd selected a child, the child nodded assent, and the agreement was sealed. It is hard to imagine a child who was tired from the trip and confused by the strange surroundings refusing anyone who promised a home. No one checked to find out whether or not each home was a good one, so no one knows how many children were loved and how many were abused.

About this time, orphanages placed older children with families as a way of disposing of them rather than as a part of a supervised child care program. Even homes nearby were not investigated, and no one followed a case to see what was happening. Many people encouraged the placement of children in foster homes to get them away from the cold and strict life in most orphanages.

Unfortunately, the careless placement of children in these years gave foster care a bad name. As a result, many children were held in institutions for all of their childhood.

While some of the orphanages may have been good places to live, most were believed to be highly rigid. The children who lived there had little chance of developing the characteristics they needed to deal with the problems of adult life. Through the years, standards of placement for foster care were developed and there was supervision by social agencies, but this process developed slowly. One reason was that there were never enough funds to provide enough social workers.

One case of child abuse that is now famous made people more aware of the problem. In 1874, a nine-year-old girl named Mary Ellen was found chained to her bed in the home of the foster parents with whom she had been placed. Concerned neighbors in a poor, crowded section of New York City where the girl lived reported their suspicions of ill-treatment to a nurse who was in the area. The nurse discovered that the little girl was not only chained to the bedpost but she was also underfed. Her body showed signs of having been beaten during different periods of her development. The nurse and some church workers told the police and the district attorney about Mary Ellen, but they found that there was no law in New York that enabled them to take her away from her parents. She was their property and they could treat her as they wished.

On behalf of Mary Ellen, the nurse and the concerned church workers went to the Society for the Prevention of Cruelty to Animals for help. They pointed out that she was a member of the animal kingdom. The society had the right to remove animals from places where they were ill-treated, and, on this basis, they removed Mary Ellen from her home. She was taken to court on a stretcher because she was too weak to walk, but her life was saved because some people cared about her.

People who heard about Mary Ellen were shocked to realize that more was being done to protect animals from abuse than to protect children. This was partly due to the idea that no one dare invade the privacy of the home or contest the rights of parents. The Society for the Prevention of Cruelty to Children was soon organized in New York, and many other groups were formed to help abused and neglected children in other parts of the country. By the year 1900 there were 161 similar groups in the United States. This progress was only a beginning in the attempts to change the lot of victims of child abuse. Only a very small percentage of abused children were reached and these were mostly cases of severe physical abuse in which children were legally removed from parents, who were punished.

At the beginning of this century, millions of children were still working very long hours in mills, factories, and mines as well as on the farms. In the next ten to twenty years, laws were passed to protect young workers. The lowest age at which children could begin work was ten. This eventually was raised to sixteen years of age in many states. The introduction of laws that made school attendance necessary also helped to reduce child labor.

Early in the twentieth century, those trying to prevent and treat child abuse began to change their approach from the punishment of parents to help for the family. In the 1930's, the Social Security Act made some funds available for the prevention and treatment of child abuse, with emphasis on children in rural areas where other welfare services were not available. The establishment of the Children's Bureau as part of a Federal program helped to provide child protection services throughout the country. A network of public and private agencies grew in efforts to provide services such as adoption, foster care, care in institutions, day care, supportive services, and protection from abuse. The Child Welfare League of America began its work which included the setting of standards in many areas of child care.

Since children are still being abused in homes and in institutions, it is obvious that the labor and education laws and efforts to improve child welfare did not solve all the problems. For many years doctors in hospitals noticed that some young children had strange "accidents," leaving them with injuries that could not be explained.

In the year 1946, Dr. John Caffey studied the X-rays of many injured children and called attention to the cases of infants with fractured bones that did not seem to be the result of accidents. At first, he did not suggest that the parents could have been responsible, but later he did speak out about this possibility. However, child abuse was still a problem too unpleasant for many doctors to accept.

During the next fifteen years, other doctors concluded that many long-bone fractures and bruises on infants who were brought to the emergency rooms might have been caused by the action of parents. But no name was given to the problem until Dr. C. Henry Kempe expressed his concern about children he treated at the Colorado General Hospital. He became alarmed because many accidents could not be explained to his satisfaction. In just one day in November 1961 there were four children in the Colorado General Hospital who appeared to have been battered. Two of the children died in the hospital and another died after being released to its home. Dr. Kempe had observed so many cases of children who suffered from injuries that did not appear to be accidental that he suggested the term "battered child syndrome." He used this term to make people aware of what he had discovered when he contacted law officers and hospitals in various parts of the country. His work was responsible for much of the present interest in child abuse.

Even in 1968, when Dr. Kempe and Dr. Ray E. Helfer's book *The Battered Child* appeared, few people were aware of the amount of physical battering of children in the United States. This book was widely read by thousands upon thousands of people who were uninformed or who had shunned an unpleasant problem. People did not want to believe that parents would turn their anger on their own children, but an article on the battered child syndrome in a medical journal commanded the attention of doctors throughout the United States. It was no longer possible to deny the existence of child abuse.

New reporting laws were passed and experts began a new search into the true causes of child abuse. The search for causes and ways to prevent and treat child abuse continues.

Today, everyone can help to prevent the hurt.

7

Ways to Prevent
Child Abuse

Child abuse hurts everyone. Just knowing that it
may be the number one killer of children in the
United States is enough to make most people want
to do something to help prevent it. When they
realize that the abused children of today often become the juvenile delinquents and criminals of to-
morrow, even the hardhearted are moved to action.

Many abused children develop learning problems and habits that destroy emotional and physical health. Many well-known criminals, such as
John Wilkes Booth, Lee Harvey Oswald, Arthur
Bremmer, Sirhan Sirhan, and James Earl Ray,
were abused as children. No one knows exactly
how much child abuse contributes to crimes, but
according to one study, 80 percent of the people
who are sent to jails and prisons for serious crimes
were abused or neglected as children. Criminals,

alcoholics, and other drug addicts are a burden to society. No wonder it can be said that child abuse hurts everyone. The cost to society can never be fully counted. No wonder the people who care only about their taxes join the people who are concerned for the lives of innocent children in asking, "What can I do?"

Until recently, it was common to avoid looking at the problem just by blaming the parents who abuse their children. If one considers parents to be the only ones responsible for their actions, it is easy to turn away. Today, there is more awareness of the big picture. While the parents must bear part of the blame, experts see that society is responsible too. Under a certain combination of circumstances, anyone could abuse or neglect a child.

Many experts see child abuse as a problem of the powerful over the powerless. They compare it with society's failure to meet the needs of people who are emotionally ill, unemployed, mentally retarded, or discriminated against for still other reasons. These people, whose self-esteem is usually low, may have great difficulty in holding others in high esteem, and these others include their own children. Parents with high self-esteem are more able to provide love and affection, while parents with low self-esteem are more likely to lash out at their children.

People may shy away from the problem of child abuse because they feel guilty about the plight of the powerless and the way society neglects them. For example, society allows or ignores terrible conditions in mental hospitals; people turn away from the problems of migrant workers, they ignore the problems of the elderly poor, and so forth. The person who abuses a child is only another example of the powerful doing terrible things to the powerless. Since society and everyone in it is more or less responsible for these situations, some of the anger people feel for the abusing parent may be anger they feel for themselves. Many young people do not feel this anger, and young people may be the very ones who can play a big part in helping to prevent child abuse. They know that preventing child abuse is far more than reporting the tragic case of a single child, important as that may be. Young people can help to promote improved policies concerning health, unemployment, welfare, and other social issues that affect the quality of life of children. Young people can make people aware of the hurt children who cry softly.

Certainly, children in the United States have come a long way in the two centuries since the American Revolution. Fewer boys and girls die from starvation and disease, fewer children labor for their keep, and almost all parents consider their children to have some rights. New agencies and laws help to protect the rights of children, but they do not reach them all.

The number of children who are abused is far greater than it needs to be. Millions of children are in desperate trouble because they are experiencing severe and frequent violence in their homes. Millions more are suffering from forms of abuse other than physical.

Young people are helping to make the public aware of the extent of child abuse by their letters to newspapers, by spreading the word to adults and friends in conversations, and by getting the interest of groups who can persuade radio and television stations to carry short announcements on the subject. Organizations listed at the end of this book can provide ideas.

Suppose you read an article in the paper about an abused child. For example, late in September of 1979, *The New York Times* printed an account of a little girl about eight years old who was found about five blocks from her home at four o'clock in the morning. She was underfed, dressed in ragged clothing, and seemed deeply frightened. She would not, or could not, talk, and her muscles were in such poor condition that she could not walk. There were cigarette burns and belt marks on her body.

When the grandmother and the mother visited the girl in the hospital after recognizing her from a television report, she showed no sign of knowing them.

If it had not been for a phone call by a person who did not give a name, the little girl might not have been found. But someone reported the abused child and, in this way, made help available.

When you read an article like this, you will find that community interest is greater than at other times. Readers of the article will be more concerned about all child abuse, so it is a good time to write to your local newspaper about the problem. You might wish to call attention to such points as:

> The seriousness of child abuse and neglect in the United States. Most people have no idea that it is one of the leading causes of death for children.

> Both parents and children are the victims of child abuse. Punishing parents turns them away from seeking sources of help. Both children and parents need help.

> About 90 percent of all child abuse is treatable. There are many ways in which parents can obtain help even without telling their names. (Suggestions are described in the next chapter.)

> Child abuse happens in all kinds of families.

> The International Labor Organization reports that the use of child labor throughout the

world is increasing. More than fifty-five million children under fifteen years of age are being used as workers. Most of them are underpaid. Many work long hours in jobs that are hazardous or harmful to their health.

These are just a few facts that can be included in a letter or a radio spot. You may wish to choose one idea and encourage groups to make posters that can spread the message in your community. Sometimes local printers will donate their services. Use short messages, such as "CHILD ABUSE HURTS EVERYONE." Anyone can print this on a poster and tack it in a place where many people will see it.

One of the important ways to help prevent child abuse is supporting and encouraging research into the causes. What does the rooming-in of newborn babies in hospitals have to do with child abuse prevention? The answer to this question is just one example of how research can help. In this case, rooming-in may help to break the cycle of child abuse as soon as babies are born.

Experiments show that parents and a newborn infant feel intense emotion when they interact physically right after birth. This is known as bonding. It appears to be important for the development of the babies and it increases attachment of the parent to the child. When parent-infant bonding

self or herself, help your friend to understand that one unpleasant or poor quality does not make a whole bad person.

Many children who are bossy, pushy, and overbearing are attempting to cover up their feelings of being worthless. People search for feelings of warmth, approval, closeness, and other good feelings in many ways. If parents do not supply them, they use various defenses in their search for them. Often, these defenses lead to further feelings of low self-esteem. Such persons make other people like them even less.

Karen's mother and father have the characteristics of many child abusers. They are too involved with their own needs to supply the support Karen needs, and Karen senses their rejection. She is the target of their abuse when their stress becomes too great. Karen finds that eating produces a good feeling, so she turns to food when her parents take their troubles out on her. She has eaten so much that she is very, very fat, and she hates herself. But the more she hates herself, the more she eats. Her parents make fun of her because she is so fat. So the cycle continues.

Since Karen is different from most people in her class, the others tease her. Perhaps if they accepted her for the many good qualities she has and encouraged her so that she felt better about herself, she would not have to stuff herself every time she felt upset. She would be less lonely, and she would not have to eat to make up for her lonely feelings.

Knowing that people can be mean because they are covering up feelings of low self-esteem can help you to get along with them. By yourself, you may not be able to break the cycle of child abuse in a case like Karen's, but everything you do to boost someone's self-esteem helps. If enough small actions are added together, they can make a big change in the big picture.

Some people say that good parenting is just a question of doing what comes naturally. For those who have consciously or unconsciously learned good parenting skills, this may work very well. But to a father who has no idea of what to expect at various ages, spanking, for example, may seem fitting for a six-month-old who is not toilet trained. Even though all children are different, many parents need to learn what to expect and not to expect from a child at various ages.

Learning how to teach young children is a part of parenting that is often neglected, and such ignorance may play a part in child abuse. For example, many mothers think that the best way to teach a baby not to bite is to bite the baby back. They think the baby will find out how much biting hurts and so will stop, but the child is more apt to learn that Mother can hurt.

The use of violence as a form of teaching is

widespread and is found in many school systems, but many experts believe that violence increases child abuse. This does not mean that a child who is spanked will necessarily become a child abuser, but spanking does teach violence as a way of life. Abusive and neglectful behavior is a complicated pattern of parenting. Besides the childhood experiences of the parent, it is caused by many other things.

Everyone can help to prevent child abuse by learning as much as possible about getting along with people and especially about being a parent. Perhaps you can convince a teacher or administrator in your school to teach a course on the subject of parenting.

Many people who want to help prevent child abuse have joined together in organizations that share this same purpose. One of these is the National Committee for the Prevention of Child Abuse. (The address is listed in "To Find Out More" at the end of this book.) This group was formed in 1972 by Donna J. Stone as a result of her concern about the increasing number of deaths due to child battering and neglect. At that time, most programs were concerned with the injured child after the abuse had occurred. The National Committee was formed to help prevent abuse *before* it occurs.

Those who join the National Committee for the

Prevention of Child Abuse pay a small annual membership fee that supports the work of this non-profit organization and provides them with copies of a newsletter, *Caring.* This keeps them abreast of current news.

The National Committee is working to make more people aware of the amount, causes, nature, and effects of child abuse, to develop prevention programs, and to encourage changes aimed at prevention. They try to communicate with concerned citizens about research, public policy, and prevention programs. They want to establish cooperation among interested organizations.

Another concerned national organization is the American Humane Association. This group was established in 1877 with the main goal of preventing cruelty, especially to children. It seeks to inform the public on the nature and extent of child abuse, child neglect, and the exploitation of children. It also tries to promote understanding about the causes of these conditions and to advise on ways to identify children who need protection. The AHA promotes services meeting the needs of abused children, organizes new programs to protect children, and improves programs already started.

The American Humane Association publishes many pamphlets about child abuse. You can learn about them and about annual membership by writing to the association. The address is given in "To Find Out More."

The United States Government provides funds for identifying, preventing, and treating child abuse. These are distributed through the National Center on Child Abuse and Neglect, a part of the Office of Child Development of the Department of Health, Education, and Welfare in Washington, D.C. The National Center is divided into ten regional resource centers that provide assistance to the states within their region. At times, free booklets on child abuse are available from them. The addresses of these centers are given in "To Find Out More."

The Child Welfare League of America is a group of child welfare agencies in the United States and Canada. Supported by private funds, this group works toward improvement of care and services for deprived, neglected, and dependent children, youth, and their families. A publications list is available for those who want further information. See "To Find Out More" for the address.

The National Center for the Prevention and Treatment of Child Abuse and Neglect in Denver, Colorado, is mainly concerned with the development of new programs for the mistreated child and his or her family. Therefore, it does not offer materials that are helpful to young people who want to work in this area, but no list of national organizations concerned with child abuse is complete without some mention of the outstanding work of this center.

There are many programs in local areas that are concerned with the big picture of the prevention of child abuse. You may discover some when you contact one of the groups that are described in the next chapter.

If you find people who believe that child abuse is a small problem that has been getting too much attention, you might tell them about Dr. Ray E. Helfer's booklet *Child Abuse: A Plan for Prevention,* written for the National Committee for the Prevention of Child Abuse. He suggests that child abuse is an epidemic that can be compared with the poliomyelitis epidemic during 1959. During that epidemic there were 5,500 reported cases. There are probably many more than a million cases of child abuse each year. Even though there is no way to stop child abuse by medicine, as in the case of polio, prevention is possible.

Helping to prevent child abuse by attacking the big picture is just one approach to the problem. You may be more interested in helping individuals or groups of people in your community to break the cycle of child abuse.

8

Help for the Child
Who Cries Softly

The voices of thousands of abused children who cry softly are now being heard by teachers, doctors, nurses, neighbors, and friends at school. Would you know what to do if a friend told you about something that had happened to him or her that seemed to be an obvious case of abuse? Would you decide to stay away from that situation, since it was none of your business? Or would you report it?

Reporting can be scary. You may wonder if someone will blame you for telling tales. But if you are certain that a person is being abused, you should report it. Do not try to solve the problem yourself. Both the abused child and the parents need help from people who are trained to provide that kind of help.

If you think you should report a case of child abuse, be certain that you know the facts, then act. Many young people who know about a case of abuse find it helpful to share the problem with a parent, teacher, religious leader, or someone they feel will understand. If a person does not want to get involved, you might remind him or her that no one can be sued for reporting a case of child abuse if it is done in good faith. You have a responsibility to see that a report is made if you know someone is being abused.

If no one will help you, or if the person you ask to help you does not know where to report child abuse, look in the yellow pages of your telephone book under the subject Social Service Organizations, or in the white pages under Child Abuse Services. Perhaps your community has a child abuse hotline. If you cannot find any of these, try the Children's Protective Services, the local welfare department, or public health authorities.

All fifty states have reporting laws. In some states it is against the law for certain people, such as doctors, dentists, teachers, and police, to ignore child abuse. Suppose a mother calls her doctor in the middle of the night because her daughter has come crying to her with an account of the father's fondling her in a way that made her feel uncomfortable. His physical affection for his child spilled over in the form of sexual contact. The mother is shocked, but she knows that her husband is sexually attracted to young children. Unlike many wives, she wants to protect her daughter, even if it means creating a problem between herself and her husband. The doctor asks to see the father at once, and he talks with him about the problem. He also mentions that he must report this case of child abuse and that the report will bring a visit from a social worker. He explains that his action is necessary by law, but this does not mean that the child will be taken from her home. It does mean that a social worker will work with him to help him overcome his problem.

Even if you do not wish to report a case of abuse, you may be interested in finding out what the reporting laws are in your state. To do this, write to the Attorney General's Office at your state capitol building. The State Department of Welfare or Public Health may be able to provide you with some information on reporting abuse in your state.

One way to help children who are being abused is to make people aware of the need for reporting and let them know how to go about making a report. In one community, an awareness program increased the amount of reporting tremendously. But increased reporting can be a problem if there are not enough services to help the children and their parents.

What happens when a case of child abuse is reported? This depends on a number of things, but especially on the kind of help that is available in a community.

Take Jane, for example. A neighbor reported that a child was being abused and a social worker came to the house to check on the truth of the report. Jane was frightened when the stranger came, even though the social worker tried to make friends with her. Jane's mother started to cry. She told the worker that the cut on Jane's face came from an accident when Jane fell with a knife in her hand. Jane knew this was not so, but if she told the strange lady the truth, her father would certainly hurt her more. Besides, she loved her father and she did not want to get him in trouble.

Suppose the police would take her father to jail if they knew the truth! Suppose they would take Jane away from her parents! This would upset Jane far more than the cut on her face that her father had made with his penknife.

The social worker told Jane that she had come to help. She promised that she would try to teach Jane's father better ways of dealing with his anger. He would not be punished if he cooperated. The social worker said that she wanted to make life better for the whole family. Jane knew that her father often became angry, and he had lashed out at her many times. She did not want to hurt her father, but she had been thinking about running away. Jane, who had never learned how to trust, did not really trust this new person. But then, she was afraid to stay home and she was afraid to run away. Maybe it was worth the chance to trust the lady who came to the house.

The social worker suggested that Jane's father join a self-help group known as Parents Anonymous. Jane had heard about this group from announcements on the radio. She had asked her father to join several months ago, but he would not talk to her about it. Now there were booklets that explained what happened at the meetings. Now he had to go or face going to court for child abuse.

Parents Anonymous is a self-help group for abusive parents that was begun in 1970 by a woman known as Jolly K., a child abuser, and Leonard Lieber, a mental health worker who was trying to help her. This organization has grown to include thousands of members in more than eight hundred chapters throughout the United States and in several other countries. The program features group meetings with a professional who volunteers to serve as a group adviser. Services are available to members twenty-four hours a day as a means of preventing child abuse. If you cannot locate a chapter in your community, or if you know people who would like to start a new chapter, write to the national headquarters of Parents Anonymous at 22330 Hawthorne Boulevard, Suite 208, Torrance, Calif. 90505. Or, if you know a parent who needs help and you cannot reach anyone, tell him or her to call one of these toll-free numbers: outside California 1-800-421-0353; in California 1-800-352-0386.

Jane's father attends a meeting of Parents Anonymous every Tuesday evening at the local Y. Many of the people who go to the meetings do not give their names, but they all talk freely about their problems. Here Jane's father is learning how to redirect his anger. Instead of hitting Jane, he pounds on chairs, hits the wall, and screams at the window when he explodes inside. He is trying not to discipline Jane when he is angry. He has learned to wait several hours, then he is calm enough to discipline her without losing control.

One of Jane's father's problems was not being able to reach out for help. After several meetings of Parents Anonymous, he became more comfortable and exchanged phone numbers with other members. Now he can contact others in the group, when he is upset, to talk with them about his feelings and to cool his anger. Sometimes he calls after he has handled a problem especially well, and each success makes the next one easier.

Jane's father is learning to look at himself differently and to repair the emotional damage that has been a burden to him for many years. Through Parents Anonymous, he and thousands of other people are improving their self-image, and this in turn improves their relationship with their children.

Parents find their way to Parents Anonymous through many routes. Some, such as Jane's father, are sent by doctors, social workers, or others because they have been reported as child abusers. Many parents join voluntarily after hearing about the group on television and/or radio. Some are referred by public and private agencies, such as the courts, police, and child protection agencies. Others hear of it through neighbors, friends, and/or relatives. In many cases, the group adviser or sponsor helps persons to reach additional services like welfare assistance, family counseling, or others that they did not know about or were afraid to reach out for.

Parents Anonymous is praised highly by experts in the field of child abuse as well as by its members. It is a way of sharing angry feelings with others and of receiving suggestions about how to act. This costs nothing and does not risk exposure. It has helped to break the cycle of abuse in thousands of families.

Hotlines are another source of help for the child who cries quietly. Besides being a way of reporting for people who become aware of abuse, they serve many parents who report their own problems. A hotline is a way of getting help without having to give one's name, but many parents do identify themselves to an understanding listener.

The hotline listener is trained to listen to an

abusive parent without being critical. For example, a parent feels she is losing control. She knows that if her daughter, Judy, upsets one more thing, she will throw her across the room. Judy's mother calls the hotline number, and the person who answers says she knows how upsetting children can be. The hotline worker listens to the mother without cutting her off or shutting her out. She really hears how the mother feels and knows what she is thinking. As she talks out her anger and frustration, Judy's mother feels calmer. A few minutes later, when Judy upsets her cup of milk, her mother calmly gives her a sponge and suggests that her daughter wipe it up. Then she pours her another glass of milk, and she feels good about herself because she kept the situation under control.

Hotline workers play a large part in referring callers to community groups such as Parents Anonymous where they can find long-term help. It takes a long time to develop a better sense of self, and this is one of the goals for preventing child abuse.

Helplines are modeled after hotlines, but they are especially concerned with the children. Many helplines are part of programs at hospitals. Most of them have volunteers who can visit a home where there is a life-threatening situation. Others will contact a rescue squad, police, or similar protective services.

Some communities have family outreach centers that work with people who seem to have a high risk for child abuse and neglect. One of their functions is to act as a support in times of tension and stress.

Crisis care centers are safe shelters for children who have been abused or are in immediate danger due to a family crisis. Children are usually placed in such a center for about two to four days. During this time, social workers and others can arrange a long-term plan of help for parents, and they can work to relieve the immediate tension. Crisis nurseries are open twenty-four hours a day so that a parent can leave a child there when the family is going through stress.

Crises and stress are common in the lives of all parents. Housing problems, unemployment, family arguments, separation from loved ones, and many other things can cause crises. Self-confidence, imagination, and knowing how to get help are some of the qualities that many child abusers lack. The occurrence of a crisis may be the last straw that pushes an already overwhelmed parent into a situation of abusing a child. Helping to relieve stress in the lives of parents is an important way in which young people can help to prevent child abuse.

When does discipline become child abuse? Dr. Catherine Chilman, professor at the School of Social Welfare, University of Wisconsin at Milwaukee, suggests that parents who are upset find it much harder to be loving but firm with children. She urges that parents get enough rest, enjoyment, and companionship for themselves. Unfortunately, many parents who abuse their children have never learned how to enjoy themselves.

Studies show that mothers who must be with their children constantly are more likely to react negatively toward them than mothers who have regular relief from their responsibilities as parents. Mothers are more likely to "blow hot and cold" with their children when they are confined with them over long periods of time.

How can you help prevent child abuse by relieving stress? Check with the family agencies in your community to see if there is a crisis nursery or day care center where you can work as a volunteer. Even if a day care center is for all children, you may help to prevent mistreatment by providing some relief for a mother who might become an abuser.

Young volunteers in day care centers may help to prevent abuse for reasons other than the relief to overburdened parents. Dr. Jill Korban, a consultant on child abuse and neglect, feels there would be advantages in building day care centers and elementary schools side by side. If school children were involved in the care of younger children, it could help develop their own self-esteem. It would also give them practice for their future role as adults and parents. It would help to educate them about normal child development with its many individual differences. And it would provide parents with a source of help in their job as care-takers, relieving them from their constant responsibility.

Some organizations provide opportunities for young people to help on an individual basis. Big Brothers/Big Sisters of America is a national organization that is acutely aware of the problems faced by families under stress. Volunteers work with children and young people who are in need of friendship and guidance, and these volunteers have the support of trained social workers. If you are interested in helping in this way, or if you feel that a Big Brother or Big Sister could help you, call the local agency listed in your telephone directory or your local social service agency.

Julie belongs to a group that works to prevent child abuse by forming relationships with individuals. She visits with Mary, a five-year-old girl whose mother used shaking as a form of discipline. Whenever it became too hard for Mary's mother to deal calmly with a situation, she shook Baby Mary very hard. Mary's mother did not know that the brain inside a baby's head is not securely anchored. Now, Mary has a vision problem because of the severe shaking.

Mary's mother never meant to hurt her baby. She was proud of the fact that she never hit her. She was only one of thousands of parents who do not realize that shaking is dangerous for young children and may result in brain damage, and/or impaired vision. Now, Mary's mother is getting help from a social worker, and she has some time to herself so that she can unwind. When Julie comes, she takes Mary for walks, plays with her in the neighborhood park, and enjoys many happy hours with the little girl every week. Julie looks forward to the eager greetings and the love that Mary gives her.

No matter how you choose to help prevent child abuse, you can be certain that your help is badly needed. Community programs vary from none to very good, but even in cities with the finest programs in the world, only a limited number of abused children and their families can be helped by them. One outstanding approach to the treatment of child abuse is a program that began at the New York Foundling Hospital in 1973, where Dr. Vincent J. Fontana did some excellent pioneering. There, a mother and her abused child live together at the Foundling's Temporary Shelter, while a team of well-trained experts bring together many skills to help break the cycle of violence. Women learn how to be good mothers through actual demonstrations, while at the same time, they themselves experience some of the mothering that they missed when they were children. In this program, mothers and children live at the hospital from three to six months. After that, members of the hospital staff keep in close touch with the family as they begin to live their lives again in the community.

Some of the mistreated children who live in the area of Denver, Colorado, are part of an outstanding program. There, at the National Center for the Prevention and Treatment of Child Abuse and Neglect, famous expert Dr. C. Henry Kempe directs activities that draw visitors from far parts of the world. Among the projects are live-in programs, a twenty-four-hour crisis nursery, a play school for abused children that is in session six hours a day, and a program with people who have been successful parents and who are willing to make home visits to parents who need support.

Education and training for doctors, nurses, social workers, and others who can help is a part of the Denver program. There are thousands of social welfare departments throughout the United States and many of them are finding help through the National Center's publications.

In one recent year, 14,473 children received help for family physical abuse in 163 programs in the United States. There is no count of how many children received help through organizations that deal with prevention and treatment of other kinds of abuse. This figure is probably very large.

One thing is certain. There is an urgent need for more people to listen for the child who cries softly and for more people to become involved with the problem of child abuse in general. You can help to make people aware that child abuse hurts everyone.

To Find
Out More

American Humane Association
5351 S. Roslyn Street
Englewood, CO 80111

Big Brothers/Big Sisters of America
117 S. 17th Street, Suite 1200
Philadelphia, PA 19103

Child Welfare League of America
67 Irving Place
New York, NY 10003

National Center on Child Abuse and Neglect
Regional Resource Centers
  Region I CA/N Resource Center
  Judge Baker Guidance Center
  295 Longwood Avenue
  Boston, MA 02115
  For: Connecticut, Maine, Massachusetts, Rhode Island,
    Vermont, New Hampshire

92

Region II CA/N Resource Center
College of Human Ecology
Cornell University
MVR Hall
Ithaca, NY 14853
For: New Jersey, New York, Puerto Rico, Virgin Islands

Region III CA/N Resource Center
Howard University Institute for Urban Affairs and Research
P.O. Box 191
Washington, DC 20059
For: District of Columbia, Delaware, Maryland, Pennsylvania, Virginia, West Virginia

Region IV CA/N Resource Center
Regional Institute for Social Welfare Research
P.O. Box 152
Athens, GA 30601
For: Alabama, Florida, Georgia, Kentucky, Mississippi, North Carolina, South Carolina, Tennessee

Region V CA/N Resource Center
Graduate School of Social Work
University of Wisconsin at Milwaukee
Milwaukee, WI 53201
For: Illinois, Indiana, Michigan, Minnesota, Ohio, Wisconsin

Region VI CA/N Resource Center
Graduate School of Social Work
University of Texas at Austin
Austin, TX 78712
For: Arkansas, Louisiana, New Mexico, Oklahoma, Texas

Region VII CA/N Resource Center
Institute of Child Behavior and Development
University of Iowa—Oakdale Campus
Oakdale, IA 52319
For: Iowa, Kansas, Missouri, Nebraska

Region VIII CA/N Resource Center
National Center for the Prevention and Treatment of
  Child Abuse and Neglect
1205 Oneida Street
Denver, CO 80220
For: Colorado, Montana, North Dakota, South Dakota,
  Utah, Wyoming

Region IX CA/N Resource Center
Department of Special Education
California State University
5151 State University Drive
Los Angeles, CA 90032
For: Arizona, California, Hawaii, Nevada, Guam

Region X CA/N Resource Center
Western Federation for Human Services
157 Yesler Way, #208
Seattle, WA 98104
For: Alaska, Idaho, Oregon, Washington

National Committee for the Prevention of Child Abuse
332 South Michigan Avenue, Suite 1250
Chicago, IL 60604

Parents Anonymous
National Headquarters
22330 Hawthorne Boulevard, Suite 208
Torrance, CA 90505

About the Author

MARGARET O. HYDE is author of an outstanding list of books for young people including *My Friend Wants to Run Away; Addictions: Gambling, Smoking, Cocaine Use, and Others; Fears and Phobias; Know About Drugs; Crime and Justice in Our Time;* and *Suicide: The Hidden Epidemic,* with Elizabeth H. Forsyth. Mrs. Hyde has written documentaries for NBC-TV and taught children, young adults, and adults.

In preparing CRY SOFTLY! THE STORY OF CHILD ABUSE, Margaret Hyde had the help of a wide variety of people, including abused children, their parents, doctors who work with these people, and persons in organizations that research this subject.

Index